Grandad
You're the Best!

THIS IS A PRION BOOK

First published in Great Britain in 2016 by Prion
An imprint of the Carlton Publishing Group
20 Mortimer Street
London W1T 3JW

Copyright 2016 © Carlton Publishing Group

A CIP catalogue for this book is available from the British Library.

ISBN 978-1-85375-950-5

Printed in Dubai

10 9 8 7 6 5 4 3 2 1

Grandad
You're the Best!

Humorous and Inspirational Quotes
Celebrating Brilliant Grandfathers

PRION

Contents

Introduction

All grandads are different, but every grandad is special and every grandad's relationship with their grandchildren is unique. Built on kindness, stories, laughter and most of all love, that bond between the generations can sustain and inspire – and can be the source of a certain amount of mischief and mayhem, too! Thank heaven for grandads!

This collection of quotations from wits, sages and celebrities across the ages salutes the grandfather in all his incarnations. From ancient Greek philosophers to modern day stand-up comedians, these observers celebrate the devotion, sense of humour and even the bemusement of our beloved grandads.

Grandad Is...

"The truly enchanting thing about small children is that they don't insist on showing you photographs of their grandparents."

Niall Toibin

"Being a grandfather is one of the true joys of life; it is an awesome time."

Catherine Pulsifer

"When I was a boy, the Dead Sea was only sick."

George Burns

"What is more enchanting than the voices of young people when you can't hear what they are saying?"

Logan Pearsall Smith

"Perfect love sometimes does not come until the first grandchild."

Welsh proverb

"Grandparents, like heroes, are as necessary to a child's growth as vitamins."

Joyce Allston

"All parents are an embarrassment
to their kids. Often, grandparents
are the relief. Kids don't have
to resist you."

Anne Lamott

"I'm not the lovable, wonderful,
tender-hearted grandfather
that you read about in books.
I'm grouchy and curmudgeonly,
and I have a lot of rules."

Pat Conroy

"What a wonderful day it is for grandad-baiting – stick a rabbit and a ferret down his trousers and see how long it is before his eyes cross."

Ken Dodd

"If it weren't for the fact that the TV set and the refrigerator are so far apart, some of us wouldn't get any exercise at all."

Joey Adam

"The best babysitters, of course,
are the baby's grandparents.
You feel completely comfortable
entrusting your baby to them for
long periods, which is why most
grandparents flee to Florida."

Dave Barry

"Something magical happens when
parents turns into grandparents.
Their attitude changes from
'money-doesn't-grow-on-trees'
to spending it like it does."

Paul Linden

"A grandfather is someone you can look up to no matter how tall you grow."

Anon

"Sometimes our grandmas and grandpas are like grand-angels."

Lexie Saige

"Why should we do anything for posterity? What has posterity ever done for us."

Joseph Addison

"One becomes a grandfather and one sees the world a little differently. Certainly the world becomes a more vulnerable place when one has a grandchild, or now I have two. And I think that possibly there's some tenderness that came out of just time and age and being a parent and grandparent."

C. K. Williams

"Grandparenthood is one of life's rewards for surviving your own children."

Anon

"Insanity is hereditary; you can
get it from your children."

Sam Levenson

"To a small child, the perfect
grandad is unafraid of big dogs
and fierce storms, but absolutely
terrified of the word 'Boo!'"

Robert Brault

"Inside every 70-year old
is a 35-year old asking,
'What happened?'"

Ann Landers

The
Best Job
in the
World

"For those of you who don't have grandchildren, get some. Get them on eBay if you have to."

Diahann Carroll

"I get to do the thing of come in and have a great time for a few hours or maybe overnight on occasion. But hey, it's almost like parenthood fantasy camp: you have all the fun without any of the long nights."

Tom Hanks

"The birth of a grandchild is a wonderful and exciting event! That wonder and excitement continues throughout life."

Tom Potts

"I love being granddaddy – Granddaddy Jim. I just get a lot of joy, a lot of joy from that little boy."

Jim Carrey

"Whenever I see my grandkids
I have an uncontrollable urge to
fling open my arms, excitedly shout
their name and scoop them up."

Jill Davis

"What a bargain grandchildren
are! I give them my loose change
and they give me a million dollars'
worth of pleasure."

Gene Perret

"I have never once regretted missing a business opportunity so that I could be with my children and grandchildren."

Mitt Romney

"One of the most powerful handclasps is that of a new grandbaby around the finger of a grandfather."

Joy Hargrove

"No cowboy was ever faster on the draw than a grandparent pulling a baby picture out of a wallet."

Anon

"I'm going to be your grandpa! I have the biggest smile. I've been waiting to meet you for such a long, long while."

Billy Crystal

"To be able to watch your
children's children grow up is
truly a blessing from above."

Byron Pulsifer

"To become a grandparent is to
enjoy one of the few pleasures in
life for which the consequences
have already been paid."

Robert Brault

"To show a child what has once delighted you, to find the child's delight added to your own, so that there is now a double delight seen in the glow of trust and affection – this is happiness."

J. B. Priestley

"Nobody can do for little children what grandparents do. Grandparents sort of sprinkle stardust over the lives of little children."

Alex Haley

"Now that I'm a grandfather myself,
I realize that the best thing about
having grandkids is that you get the
kid for the best part of the ride –
kind of like owning a car for only
the first 10,000 miles. You can have
your grandchildren for a couple
of days and then turn them back
over to the parents."

Willard Scott

"If I had known how wonderful it
would be to have grandchildren,
I'd have had them first."

Lois Wyse

"The best place to be when you're
sad is grandpa's lap."

Anon

"Surely, two of the most satisfying
experiences in life must be those of
being a grandchild or a grandparent."

Donald A. Norberg

"Some of the world's best
educators are grandparents."

Charles W. Shedd

"I have been described as the
grandfather of climate change.
In fact, I am just a grandfather
and I do not want my grandchildren
to say that grandpa understood
what was happening but didn't
make it clear."

James Hansen

"There are fathers who do not love
their children; there is no grandfather
who does not adore his grandson."

Victor Hugo

"Being grandparents sufficiently
removes us from the responsibilities
so that we can be friends."

Allan Frome

"Children's children are
a crown to the aged."

Proverbs 17:6

"Few things are more delightful than
grandchildren fighting over your lap."

Doug Larson

"Every generation revolts against
its fathers and makes friends
with its grandfathers."

Lewis Mumford

"Everyone needs to have access both
to grandparents and grandchildren
in order to be a full human being."

Margaret Mead

"A grandchild fills a space
in your heart that you never
knew was empty."

Anon

"Check that out, a grandfather!
Strange how life works. One day
you are in a haze, the next you
are a family man."

Steven Tyler

"Get ready to fall completely in love again... Get ready to be like the lowest person in the pecking order in your family."

George W. Bush

"A baby boy has a special way of bringing out the man in his father and the little boy in his grandfather."

Tanya Masse

"I can just look at her now and make a sound and she lights up. It's better than any spotlight I've ever been in."

Billy Crystal

"If a child is to keep alive his inborn sense of wonder, he needs the companionship of at least one adult who can share it, rediscovering with him the joy, excitement and mystery of the world we live in."

Rachel Carson

"If we fail here, we fail humanity...
As a grandfather, I have no
intention of failing my, or anyone
else's, grandchildren."

Prince Charles

"Our grandchildren accept us
for ourselves, without rebuke or
effort to change us, as no one in
our entire lives has ever done,
not our parents, siblings, spouses,
friends – and hardly ever our own
grown children."

Ruth Goode

The Art of
Grandparenting

"How do you know someone is a grandparent? They've got milk stains on every shirt from burping babies. Their pants are worn out at the knees from crawling around giving pony rides. They have 2,842 pictures of the grandkids on their smart phone and not one photo of their spouse."

Regina Brett

"What advice do I tell my grandson? I listen to him."

Roy Haynes

"Because [grandparents] are usually free to love and guide and befriend the young without having to take daily responsibility for them, they can often reach out past pride and fear of failure and close the space between generations."

Jimmy Carter

"A child needs a grandparent, anybody's grandparent, to grow a little more securely into an unfamiliar world."

Charles and Ann Morse

"The reason grandchildren and
grandparents get along so well is
that they have a common enemy."

Sam Levenson

"Life is a country that the old have
seen and lived in. Those who have
to travel through it can only learn
the way from them."

Joseph Joubert

"It is easier to build strong children
than to repair broken men."

Frederick Douglass

"Children have never been very good at listening to their elders, but they have never failed to imitate them."

James Baldwin

"Well-being changes as we move through life, which is why a child's version of it cannot be the same as an old person's."

Deepak Chopra

"What children need most are
the essentials that grandparents
provide in abundance. They give
unconditional love, kindness,
patience, humour, comfort, lessons in
life. And, most importantly, cookies."

Rudy Giuliani

"The great thing about getting
older is that you get a chance to tell
the people in your life who matter
what they mean to you."

Mike Love

"What I and many grandparents
have discovered is that when it
comes to advice, less is more.
The less you volunteer your
opinions, the more you seem
to be asked for them."

Gloria Hunniford

"When is your grandpa's bedtime?
Three hours after he falls asleep
on the couch."

Anon

"Growing old is mandatory;
growing up is optional."

Chili Davis

"Don't let them challenge you,
don't let them intimidate you…
And you do your thing.
That's the only way to do it."

Ariana Grande's grandfather

"Hugs can do great amounts of
good – especially for children."

Princess Diana

"It's sad that grandkids show up at the end of obituaries, way behind the list of workplace achievements, social clubs and survivors. Why last? If you've got grandkids, you know they're first when it comes to the joy in your life."

Regina Brett

"My grandkids believe I'm the oldest thing in the world. And after two or three hours with them, I believe it, too."

Gene Perret

"Nothing is more responsible for the good old days than a bad memory."

Franklin Pierce Adams

"His grandfather had often told him that he tried too hard to move trees when a wiser man would walk around them."

Patricia Briggs

"Children need models rather than critics."

Joseph Joubert

"My grandchildren are my stake in the near future, and it's my great hope that they might one day say, 'Grandpa was part of a great movement that helped to turn things around.'"

David Suzuki

"Each child brings so much joy and hope into the world, and that is reason enough for being here. As you grow older, you will contribute something else to this world, and only you can discover what that is."

Sharon Creech

"The very fact that you don't look or act or feel like the grandparents of even a generation ago does not mean that you are less, but that you are more − in effect, an evolved form of grandparents, primed to do a bigger and more challenging job than any group before you."

Arthur Kornhaber

"If you haven't time to respond to a tug at your pants leg, your schedule is too crowded."

Robert Brault

"The most important thing my grandfather taught me was that the most noble way to use your skills, intellect and energy is to defend the marginalized against those with the greatest power – and that the resulting animosity from those in power is a badge of honour."

Glenn Greenwald

"Only where children gather is there any real chance of fun."

Mignon McLaughlin

"I loved and worshipped my grandparents… My grandfather was a highly intelligent, quiet man. He said, 'Jeff, one day you'll understand that it's harder to be kind than clever.'"

Jeff Bezos

"My grandkids always beat me at Rock Band. And I say, listen, you may beat me at Rock Band, but I made the original records, so shut up."

Paul McCartney

"A grandfather talking to his young grandson tells the boy he has two wolves inside of him struggling with each other. The first is the wolf of peace, love and kindness. The other wolf is fear, greed and hatred. 'Which wolf will win, Grandfather?' asks the young boy. 'Whichever one I feed,' is the reply."

Native American proverb

"The older a man gets, the further he had to walk to school as a boy."

Josh Billings

"As I was growing up, I always had the feeling that I understood a lot more than I knew. When I listen to my grandchildren, I think they know a lot more than they understand."

Anon

"As my Sicilian grandfather used to say, you get more flies with honey than with vinegar, right?"

Andrew Cuomo

"Old men are fond of giving good advice to console themselves for their inability to give bad examples."

François de La Rochefoucauld

"If my grandchildren were to look at me and say, 'You were aware species were disappearing and you did nothing, you said nothing,' that I think is culpable. I don't know how much more they expect me to be doing. I'd better ask them."

David Attenborough

"It is utterly false and cruelly arbitrary to put all the play and learning into childhood, all the work into middle age, and all the regrets into old age."

Margaret Mead

"I think the power of a grandchild is it taps an instinct that people later in life also have towards... the world of non-profits or charities. They want to leave a better place."

David Eisenhower

"Young men, hear an old man
to whom old men hearkened
when he was young."

Anon

"You are as young as your faith, as
old as your doubt; as young as your
self-confidence, as old as your fear;
as young as your hope, as old as
your despair."

Douglas MacArthur

Little
Treasures

"Grandchildren don't stay young
forever, which is good because
grandfathers only have so many
horsey rides in them."

Gene Perret

"I go to my grandchildren.
They keep their grandpa
informed on what's going on."

Ben Veeren

"Make no mistake about why
these babies are here; they are
here to replace us."

Jerry Seinfeld

"I love music of all kinds,
but there's no greater music
than the sound of my
grandchildren laughing."

Sylvia Earle

"Two things I dislike about my granddaughter – when she won't take her afternoon nap and when she won't let me take mine."

Gene Perret

"I'm probably a bit of a cheeky grandson, like my brother as well. We both tend to take the mickey a bit much."

Prince William, Duke of Cambridge

"Do you know why grandchildren are always so full of energy? They suck it out of their grandparents."

Gene Perret

"I'm the twinkle in my grandpa's eye..."

Anon

"I have a horror of leaving this world and not having anyone in the family know how to replace a toilet-roll holder."

Erma Bombeck

"Grandchildren give us a second chance to do things better because they bring out the best in us."

Anon

"My grandchild has taught me what true love means. It means watching *Scooby-Doo* cartoons while the basketball game is on another channel."

Gene Perret

"Lending money to your children is like lending money to a Third World country – you never get the interest back, let alone the principal."

J. L. Long

"Fathers are men who give daughters away to other men who aren't nearly good enough... so they can have grandchildren who are smarter than anybody's."

Anon

"I am convinced that grandkids are inherently evil people who tell their grandparents to 'just go to the library and open up an email account – it's free and so simple.'"

Scott Douglas

"I don't intentionally spoil my grandkids. It's just that correcting them often takes more energy than I have left."

Gene Perret

"I love all my children, but some of
them I don't like."

Lillian Carter

"Grandchildren now don't write
a thank you for the Christmas
presents. They are walking on their
pants with their cap on backward,
listening to the Enema Man and
Snoopy, Snoopy Poop Dog."

Alan Simpson

"Elephants and grandchildren
never forget."

Andy Rooney

"What is a home without
children? Quiet."

Henry Youngman

"Having a two-year-old is like
having a blender that you
don't have the top for."

Jerry Seinfeld

"As I have gotten older, I've discovered the joys of being lazy."

Julie Bowen

"By the time the youngest children have learned to keep the house tidy, the oldest grandchildren are on hand to tear it to pieces."

Christopher Morley

"People talk to old people like they're children. 'Oh you're very old aren't you?' Yeah I'm old. I'm not stupid."

Craig Ferguson

Our
Grandad

"Just lean on me Grandfather,
I'll walk very slowly."

Frances Hodgson Burnett

"I phoned my grandparents and
my grandfather said, 'We saw your
movie.' 'Which one?' I said. He
shouted, 'Betty, what was the name
of that movie I didn't like?'"

Brad Pitt

"Grampa: Unfortunately,
like all true stories, this one
has a crappy ending.
Bart: You have a story with
an ending?"

The Simpsons

"My father is a great grandfather.
He's a wonderful grandfather, but
he's a terrible husband."

Pamela Anderson

"When I was little, my grandfather used to make me stand in a closet for five minutes without moving. He said it was elevator practice."

Steven Wright

"And to the memory of my grandfather, who taught me to look up to people others looked down on, because we're not so different after all."

Bill Clinton

"When people say 'Charlie Chaplin'
I still think now of the guy in the
moustache and bowler hat and
funny walk – I don't think of an old
man who was my grandfather."

Oona Chaplin

"Grandfather was well known
for being stubborn in his ideas.
For instance, you had to go to
sleep facing east so that you
would be ready to greet the
sun when it returned."

Michael Dorris

"It's interesting that I had such
a close relationship with my
grandfather. Because your parents
always judge you. They say, 'You
shouldn't do this, you shouldn't do
that.' But with your grandparents
you have a feeling that you can say
anything or you can do anything,
and they will support you.
That's why you have this
kind of connection."

Novak Djokovic

"Look at Grandad. His brain went years ago, now his legs have gone. There's only the middle bit of him left."

Del Boy, Only Fools and Horses

"I keep lot of my opinions to myself. My grandfather, who was a gravedigger, told me one day, 'Son, the next time you go by the cemetery, remember that a third of the people are in there because they got into other people's business.'"

Lee Trevino

"I played with my grandfather a lot as a kid. He was dead, but my parents had him cremated and put his ashes in my Etch A Sketch."

Alan Harvey

"I've met the Dalai Lama briefly, but I would probably say my grandfather was the wisest person I ever met. He was my mother's father, an Indian, a family doctor and very unlike me in that he was deeply religious."

Salman Rushdie

"My grandfather had a particularly important influence on my life, even though I didn't visit him often, since he lived about three miles out of town and he died when I was six. He was remarkably curious about the world and he read lots of books."

Umberto Eco

"More and more, when I single out the person out who inspired me most, I go back to my grandfather."

James Earl Jones

"Grampa: Why are you people avoiding me? Does my withered face remind you of the grim spectre of death?
Homer: Yes, but there's more. Dad, I love you, but... you're a weird, sore-headed old crank and nobody likes you!"

The Simpsons

"When I die, I want to go peacefully like my grandfather did – in his sleep. Not yelling and screaming like the passengers in his car."

Bob Monkhouse

"Distant relatives are the best kind
and the further away the better."

Kim Hubbard

"I come from a long line of fighters.
My maternal grandfather was the
toughest guy I ever knew. World
War II veteran, killed 20 men,
and spent the rest of the war in
an Allied prison camp. My father
battled blood pressure and obesity
all his life. Different kind of fight."

Dwight Schrute

"I'll always remember the last
words of my grandfather,
who said: 'A truck!'"

Emo Philips

"I met my grandfather just before he
died and it was the first time that
I had seen dad with a relative of
his. It was interesting to see my own
father as a son and the body language
and alteration in attitude that comes
with that, and it sort of changed our
relationship for the better."

Christian Bale

"Because I would rather be with my grandfather on Alp than anywhere on earth."

Johanna Spyri, Heidi

"I'm awful at karaoke, but if I did have to sing I'd go for my favourite Frank Sinatra song 'I've Got You Under My Skin'. The fact I love Frank is my grandfather's doing: he drummed it into me from a very early age that Frank Sinatra is God."

Matt Smith

"I'm very proud of my gold pocket watch. My grandfather, on his deathbed, sold me this watch."

Woody Allen

"If I'd been born in my grandfather's time, I'd have made my grandfather's mistakes. There's no doubt of it. I just don't want to make my grandfather's mistakes today."

Frank Herbert

"My grandfather was the first person in my family to recognize that I was musical. Grandpa would take me to Times Square every Saturday afternoon where he had found a 'Record Your Own Voice' booth. For 25 cents, you could sing or talk, and they would give you a scratchy record to take home. He was a great guy. I'm sure I wouldn't be the man I've become without him."

Barry Manilow

"The history of our grandparents is remembered not with rose petals, but in the laughter and tears of their children and their children's children. It is into us that the lives of grandparents have gone. It is in us that their history becomes a future."

Charles and Ann Morse

"I was taught by my grandfather that anything that your mind can conceive, you can have. It's a reality."

Lenny Kravitz

"Marge: I'm sorry, Maggie, but growing up means giving up the things you love.
Grampa: It's true. I had to give up everything but raisins, and the doctor says even those are killing me. Sweet, plump coffin nails they are."

The Simpsons

"Dear old Grandad, bless him. He was about as useful as a pair of sunglasses on a bloke with one ear."

Del Boy, Only Fools and Horses

"My grandfather always said that
I shouldn't watch my money, that
I should watch my health. So one
day when I was watching my health,
someone stole my money.
It was my grandfather."

Jackie Mason

"My grandfather always said
that living is like licking honey
off a thorn."

Louis Adamic

"My grandfather always told me, 'Go through life with your hands in your pockets, making fists so everyone will think that they're full of money.' What he meant was that you should never let people see you down."

Ricky Martin

"My grandfather did not travel across 4,000 miles of the Atlantic Ocean to see this country overrun by immigrants. He did it because he killed a man back in Ireland."

Stephen Colbert

"My grandfather died more than 25 years ago, but I still think of him a lot and smell his smell."

Julian Clary

"My grandfather is the king, my dad's the prince, I guess that makes me the butler."

Adam Petty

"Rock's so good to me. Rock is my child and my grandfather."

Chuck Berry

"My grandfather once told me that there were two kinds of people: those who do the work and those who take the credit. He told me to try to be in the first group; there was much less competition."

Indira Gandhi

"My grandfather taught me how important it is to have your eyes open, because you never know what's going to come your way."

Bobbi Brown

"My grandfather used to say: 'Aim high, even if you hit a cabbage.' It is about having a goal or a dream and never giving up."

Baroness Tanni Grey-Thompson

"My grandfather was a giant of a man... When he walked, the earth shook. When he laughed, the birds fell out of the trees. His hair caught fire from the sun. His eyes were patches of sky."

Eth Clifford

"You come on as a guest. You don't get the girl anymore. But that is our lives. You start off as the boyfriend, then you are the lover, then you are the husband, then you are the father, and then you are the grandfather."

Albert Finney

"My grandfather was a great role model. Through him I learned the gentle side of men."

Sarah Long

There's Life in the Old Dog Yet!

"It's amazing how grandparents seem
so young once you become one."

Anon

"Just 'cause there's snow on
the roof doesn't mean there's
not a fire inside."

Bonnie Hunt

"A sexagenarian? At his age?
I think that's disgusting."

Gracie Allen

"Neil Young sang, 'It's better to
burn out than to fade away.'
I say it's better to burn slow
and see your grandkids."

Austin Kleon

"The great secret that all old people
share is that you really haven't
changed in 70 or 80 years. Your
body changes, but you don't change
at all. And that, of course, causes
great confusion."

Doris Lessing

"The longer I live the more
beautiful life becomes."

Frank Lloyd Wright

"The secret of genius is to carry
the spirit of the child into old
age, which means never
losing your enthusiasm."

Aldous Huxley

"The older the fiddler,
the sweeter the tune."

Irish proverb

"Age does not diminish the extreme disappointment of having a scoop of ice cream fall from the cone."

Jim Fiebig

"Age is an issue of mind over matter. If you don't mind, it doesn't matter."

Mark Twain

"Ageing is not lost youth, but a new stage of opportunity and strength."

Betty Friedan

"I don't want to put a pause on the rest of my life; I'm really enjoying getting older and the wisdom that comes from that."

Rosemarie DeWitt

"Inside every old person is a young person wondering what happened."

Terry Pratchett

"You can't help getting older, but you don't have to get old."

George Burns

"The great thing about getting older
is that you don't lose all the other
ages you've been."

Madeleine L'Engle

"Count your age by friends, not years.
Count your life by smiles, not tears."

John Lennon

"Don't think how old you are. Think
only of what you can accomplish.
Go! Do! This alone is living."

Peggy Mann

"Adults are just outdated children."

Dr Seuss

"I keep fit. Every morning, I do a hundred laps of an Olympic-sized swimming pool – in a small motor launch."

Peter Cook

"I will never be an old man. To me, old age is always 15 years older than I am."

Francis Bacon

"I'm hoping they slow down a
little bit with technology, because
I'm just trying to keep up."

Kate Upton

"It's not how old you are,
but how you are old."

Marie Dressler

"My doctor tells me I should start
slowing it down – but there are more
old drunks than there are old doctors,
so let's all have another round."

Willie Nelson

"Now that I'm over 60 I'm veering toward respectability."

Shelley Winters

"Old age begins when a person starts worrying about it."

Eduardo Albarracin Ramirez

"Old age is an excellent time for outrage. My goal is to say or do at least one outrageous thing every week."

Louis Kronenberger

"Someday you will be old enough to start reading fairy tales again."

C. S. Lewis

"Wisdom doesn't necessarily come with age. Sometimes age just shows up all by itself."

Tom Wilson

"Wrinkles should merely indicate where smiles have been."

Mark Twain

Keep It
in the
Family

"Holding these babies in my arms
makes me realize the miracle my
husband and I began."

Betty Ford

"There's nothing like having
a grandchild to restore faith
to heredity."

Doug Larson

"You don't choose your family.
They are God's gift to you,
as you are to them."

Desmond Tutu

"Grandparents should play the same role in the family as an elder statesman can in the government of a country. They have the experience and knowledge that comes from surviving a great many years of life's battles, and the wisdom, hopefully, to recognise how their grandchildren can benefit from this."

Geoff Dench

"Who wants to be married to a grandfather?"

Loretta Lynn

"Young people need something stable to hang on to – a culture connection, a sense of their own past, a hope for their own future. Most of all, they need what grandparents can give them..."

Jay Kesler

"We've had bad luck with our kids – they've all grown up."

Christopher Morley

"Other things may change us, but
we start and end with the family."

Anthony Brandt

"A baby is born with a need to be
loved – and never outgrows it."

Frank A. Clark

"A grandchild is a miracle, but a
renewed relationship with your own
children is even a greater one."

T. Berry Brazelton

"Family faces are magic mirrors. Looking at people who belong to us, we see the past, present and future."

Gail Lumet Buckley

"A man who doesn't spend time with his family can never be a real man."

Mario Puzo

"After a good dinner one can forgive anybody, even one's own relations."

Oscar Wilde

"People are pretty forgiving when it comes to other people's families. The only family that ever horrifies you is your own."

Douglas Coupland

"Soup is a lot like a family. Each ingredient enhances the others; each batch has its own characteristics; and it needs time to simmer to reach full flavour."

Marge Kennedy

"That is the thankless position of the father in the family – the provider for all and the enemy of all."

August Strindberg

"A happy family is but an earlier heaven."

George Bernard Shaw

"The first half of our lives is ruined by our parents and the second half by our children."

Clarence Darrow

"The baby boomers owe a big debt
of gratitude to the parents and
grandparents – who we haven't
given enough credit to anyway –
for giving us another generation."

Steven Spielberg

"The closest friends I made all
through life have been people who
also grew up close to a loved and
loving grandmother or grandfather."

Margaret Mead

"Family traditions counter alienation and confusion. They help us define who we are; they provide something steady, reliable and safe in a confusing world."

Susan Lieberman

"All the grandchildren call me Dan Dan. I don't know why. Even my children call me Dan Dan now. You name your children, then your children rename their grandparents. That's their privilege."

Tony Benn

"Few things are more satisfying than seeing your children have teenagers of their own."

Doug Larson

"In a brief space the generations of beings are changed, and, like runners, pass on the torches of life."

Lucretius

"Be kind to your kids. They'll choose your nursing home one day."

Anon

"Another good thing about being poor is that when you are 70 your children will not have you declared legally insane in order to gain control of your estate."

Woody Allen

"Grandchildren complete the circle of love."

Anon

"Grandchildren are the dots that connect the lines from generation to generation."

Lois Wyse

"If you're a good person, the goodness will continue through your descendants."

Diane von Furstenberg

"Grandkids are the kids we all should've had before we had kids."

Lou Silluzio

"Grandparents often talk about the younger generation as if they didn't have anything to do with it."

Haim Ginott

"Happiness is having a large, loving, caring, close-knit family in another city."

George Burns

"Have children while your parents are still young enough to take care of them."

Rita Rudner

"Having a baby changes the way you view your in-laws. I love it when they come to visit now. They can hold the baby and I can go out."

Matthew Broderick

"I've been called a moron since I was about four. My father called me a moron. My grandfather said I was a moron. And a lot of times when I'm driving, I hear I'm a moron. I like being a moron."

Adam Sandler

"Maybe there is no actual place
called hell. Maybe hell is just
having to listen to our grandparents
breathe through their noses when
they're eating sandwiches."

Jim Carrey

"I don't mind being a grandfather;
I've been a mother for so many
years. You just can't believe what
it's like being a father. Especially
when you come out of the chaos
of the road to getting married
and having children."

Steven Tyler

"I have learned that to be with
those I like is enough."

Walt Whitman

"I was an overly young father,
is the most polite way of putting it.
I think I was rather immature and
all I can say is that I think I've
made a much better grandfather...
I don't think I was ready to be a
father to be honest."

Michael Morpurgo

"I was born into a very important family in Japan. My grandfather was a descendant of the Emperor and we were very wealthy."

Yoko Ono

"The average American may not know who his grandfather was. But the American was, however, one degree better off than the average Frenchman who, as a rule, was in considerable doubt as to who his father was."

Mark Twain

"The bond that links your true family is not one of blood, but of respect and joy in each other's life. Rarely do members of one family grow up under the same roof."

Richard Bach

"There's nothing that makes you more insane than family. Or more happy. Or more exasperated. Or more... secure."

Jim Butcher

"They want to get back on their kids for screwing up their lives, so they're your best friends. 'You know, Grandpa, Dad's yelling at me.' 'Oh yeah? Well tell him he peed in his bed 'til he was 12. See if he yells at you now.'"

Eddie Brill

"The greatest thing in family life is to take a hint when a hint is intended – and not to take a hint when a hint isn't intended."

Robert Frost

"Without a family, man, alone in the world, trembles with the cold."

Andre Maurois

"I looked up my family tree and found out I was the sap."

Rodney Dangerfield

"In every conceivable manner, the family is link to our past, bridge to our future."

Alex Haley

"Insanity runs in my family.
It practically gallops."

Cary Grant

"To us, family means putting your arms
around each other and being there."

Barbara Bush

"The trouble about being retired is
that you never get a break from it."

Tom Farmer

"There is no such thing as fun for the whole family."

Jerry Seinfeld

"When I remember my family, I always remember their backs. They were always indignantly leaving places."

John Cheever

"Family is not an important thing. It's everything."

Michael J. Fox

Wise Words

"I would love to go back and travel
the road not taken, if I knew at
the end of it I'd find the same
set of grandkids."

Robert Brault

"Varicose veins are the result
of an improper selection
of grandparents."

William Osler

"That's right. When I was your age,
television was called books."

The Princess Bride

"Anyone who thinks the art of conversation is dead ought to tell a child to go to bed."

Robert Gallagher

"You kids today with your water. When we were kids we didn't have water. We used to suck the fluid out of mud and we were grateful for that fluid."

Dom Irerra

"You can't own a mountain any more than you can own an ocean or a piece of the sky. You hold it in trust. You live on it, you take life from it, and once you're dead, you rest in it."

Grandad Walton, *The Waltons*

"The old believe everything, the middle-aged suspect everything, the young know everything."

Oscar Wilde

"We want not so much a father but a grandfather in heaven, a god who said of anything we happened to like doing, 'What does it matter so long as they are contented?'"

C. S. Lewis

"The idea that no one is perfect is a view most commonly held by people with no grandchildren."

Doug Larson

"The joy of grandchildren is
measured in the heart."

Anon

"Youth is a wonderful thing. What a
crime to waste it on children."

George Bernard Shaw

"Youthfulness is about how you live
not when you were born."

Karl Lagerfeld

"Children are the keys of paradise."
Eric Hoffer

"Oh are there two nine o'clocks
in the day?"
Tallulah Bankhead

"By the time a man realizes that
maybe his father was right, he usually
has a son who thinks he's wrong."
Charles Wadsworth

"You have to do your own growing no matter how tall your grandfather was."

Abraham Lincoln

"You can learn many things from children. How much patience you have, for instance."

Franklin P. Jones

"The whiter my hair becomes, the more ready people are to believe what I say."

Bertrand Russell

"It is perfectly possible that a grandfather can have a more scientific mind than his grandchildren! Societies do not always go forward! Sometimes old generations are much luckier!"

Mehmet Murat Ildan

"They told me that grandchildren are the reward you get for not killing your children."

Virginia Ironside

"True love isn't Romeo and Juliet who died together, it's grandpa and grandma who grew old together."

Anon

"Children make your life important."

Erma Bombeck

"There was no respect for youth when I was young, and now that I am old, there is no respect for age – I missed it coming and going."

J. B. Priestley

"The years between 50 and 70 are the hardest. You are always being asked to do things and yet you are not decrepit enough to turn them down."

T. S. Eliot

"Advice in old age is foolish, for what can be more absurd than to increase our provisions for the road the nearer we approach to our journey's end."

Cicero

"If you want to know where I come
by the passionate commitment
I have to bringing people together
without regard to race, it all started
with my grandfather."

Bill Clinton

"By the time you're 80 you've
learned everything. Too bad you
can't remember any of it."

George Burns

"In youth the days are short and the years are long; in old age the years are short and the days long."

Nikita Ivanovich Panin

"It is one of nature's ways that we often feel closer to distant generations than to the generation immediately preceding us."

Igor Stravinsky

Were Dinosaurs Alive When You Were Young?

"Grandchildren are God's way of
compensating us for growing old."

Mary H. Waldrip

"Grandchildren don't make a man
feel old; it's the knowledge that he's
married to a grandmother."

G. Norman Collie

"You know you're getting old when you
get that one candle on the cake. It's like,
'See if you can blow this out.'"

Jerry Seinfeld

"Just remember, once you're over the hill you begin to pick up speed."

Charles Schulz

"At 60, your hair becomes a cosmic joke. It moves from your head to your ears and your nose. And you can't see it without one of those giant funhouse mirrors."

Greg Tamblyn

"Let us respect grey hairs, especially our own."

J. P. Sears

"I'm like old wine. They don't
bring me out very often – but
I'm well preserved."

Rose Kennedy

"Nod away at him Mr Pip, nod
away at him: that's what he likes."

Charles Dickens, Great Expectations

"As a man grows older he either
talks more and says less or talks
less and says more."

Anon

"First you forget names, then you forget faces, then you forget to pull your zipper up, then you forget to pull your zipper down."

Leo Rosenberg

"As a young man I used to have four supple members and one stiff one. Now I have four stiff and one supple."

Henri d'Orléans, Duke of Aumale

"At 18 you worry about what everyone thinks of you. At 40 you don't care. At 60 you realise no one was thinking about you anyway!"

Daniel G. Amen

"Better to go than sit around being a terrible old bore."

Auberon Waugh

"Everything slows down with age, except the time it takes cake and ice cream to reach your hips."

John Wagner

"Beautiful is old age – beautiful as the slow-dropping mellow autumn of a rich glorious summer. In the old man, Nature has fulfilled her work; she loads him with blessings; she fills him with the fruits of a well-spent life; and, surrounded by his children and his children's children, she rocks him softly away to a grave, to which he is followed with blessings. God forbid we should not call it beautiful."

J. A. Froude

"As you get older, your metabolism slows down. You've got to admit it. It's nothing to be ashamed of if you have lived your life to the full."

Rod Stewart

"Do not regret growing older. It is a privilege denied to many."

Anon

"Getting old is a fascinating thing. The older you get, the older you want to get."

Keith Richards

"I always have trouble remembering
three things: faces, names, and – I can't
remember what the third thing is."

Fred Allen

"As human beings we value the
experience that comes with age.
We are reminded over and over
again with statements like 'older
and wiser' and 'respect your elders,'
promoting age as something to be
cherished and respected."

Jenna Morasca

"I have reached an age when,
if someone tells me to wear socks,
I don't have to."

Albert Einstein

"As you grow old, you lose interest
in sex, your friends drift away
and your children often ignore
you. There are other advantages,
of course, but these are the
outstanding ones."

Richard Needham

"You end up as you deserve.
In old age you must put up with
the face, the friends, the health and
the children you have earned."

Judith Viorst

"I was brought up to respect my
elders, so now I don't have to
respect anybody."

George Burns

"My mother used to say: 'The older you get, the better you get, unless you're a banana.'"

Rose, The Golden Girls

"Nothing makes me feel so old as having to scroll down to find my year of birth..."

Anon

"Old age is the most unexpected of all things that can happen to a man."

Leon Trotsky

"You get old and you realize there are no answers, just stories."

Garrison Keillor

"I still have a full deck; I just shuffle slower now."

Anon

"You spend a much larger part of your life being old, not young."

Douglas Coupland

"Old age may have its limitations and challenges, but in spite of them, our latter years can be some of the most rewarding and fulfilling of our lives."

Billy Graham

"You know you are getting old when the candles cost more than the cake."

Bob Hope

"I'm getting to an age when I can only enjoy the last sport left. It's called hunting for your spectacles."

Edward Grey

"Old age, believe me, is a good and pleasant thing. It is true you are gently shouldered off the stage, but then you are given such a comfortable front stall as spectator."

Confusius

"The crucial task of old age is balance: keeping just well enough, just brave enough, just gay and interested and starkly honest enough to remain a sentient human being."

Florida Scott-Maxwell

"The elderly don't drive that badly; they're just the only ones with time to do the speed limit."

Jason Love

"To be 70 years young is sometimes far more cheerful and hopeful than to be 40 years old."

Oliver Wendell Holmes

"The first thing I do when I wake up in the morning is breathe on a mirror and hop it fogs."

Earl Wynn

"One of the good things about getting older is you find you're more interesting than most of the people you meet."

Lee Marvin

"They tell you that you'll lose your mind when you grow older. What they don't tell you is that you won't miss it very much."

Malcolm Cowley

"To get back my youth I would do anything in the world, except take exercise, get up early or be respectable."

Oscar Wilde

"When grace is joined with wrinkles, it is adorable. There is an unspeakable dawn in happy old age."

Victor Hugo